American Battlefields

GETTYSBURG

JULY 1–3, 1863

Brendan January

Enchanted Lion Books
New York

© 2004 White-Thomson Publishing Limited
and Enchanted Lion Books LLC

Published in the United States of America in 2004 by
Enchanted Lion Books, 115 West 18 Street, New York, NY 10011

Library of Congress Cataloging-in-Publication Data
January, Brendan, 1972-
Gettysburg, July 1-3, 1863 / Brendan January.
p. cm. — (American battlefields)
Includes bibliographical references (p.) and index.
ISBN 1-59270-025-X
1. Gettysburg, Battle of, Gettysburg, Pa., 1863—Juvenile literature.
[1.Gettysburg, Battle of, Gettysburg, Pa., 1863. 2. United States—
History—Civil War, 1861-1865—Campaigns.] I. Title. II. Series.
E475.53.J36 2004
973.7'349—dc22   2003064295

Created for Enchanted Lion Books by
White-Thomson Publishing Limited
Bridgewater Business Centre
210 High Street
Lewes, BN7 2UH

Titles in the series American Battlefields:
The Alamo
Gettysburg
Lexington and Concord
Little Bighorn

Editorial Credits
Editor: Peg Goldstein
Designer: Clare Nicholas, based on a series design by Jamie Asher
Consultant: Steve Mills, Ph. D., Keele University
Proofreader: Alison Cooper
Picture Research: Shelley Noronha, Glass Onion Pictures
Artwork: Peter Bull Studio

Enchanted Lion Books
Editor: Claudia Zoe Bedrick
Production: Millicent Fairhurst

Printed in China by South China Printing Company

Picture Credits
Bradley Schmehl Fine Art title page, 17; Library of Congress imprint
page, 10(b), 19(t), 19(bl), 22, 26; Missouri e-Communities, LLC 8(t),
10(b), 23(t), 29(t); National Archives Images 8(b), 13, 14(b), 16;
National Park Service/Gettysburg National Military Park cover, 25(b);
Peter Newark's American Pictures 4, 5, 7(b), 9, 11(t), 14(t), 15, 17(t),
20, 23(b), 25(t), 27(t), 27(b), 29(b); New York Historical Society 7(t),
19(br).

Disclaimer: The website addresses (URLs) included in this book were valid at
the time of going to press. However, because of the nature of the Internet, it is
possible that some addresses may have changed, or sites may have changed or
been closed down since publication. While the author, packager, and publisher
regret any inconvenience that this may cause readers, no responsibility for any
such changes can be accepted by either the author, packager, or publisher.

Every effort has been made to trace copyright holders. However, the publisher
apologizes for any unintentional omissions and would be pleased in such cases
to add an acknowledgement in any future editions.

Cover art: Pickett's Charge, from the Gettysburg Cyclorama. Courtesy of
the National Park Service/Gettysburg National Military Park.
Title page art: Bedlam in the Brickyard by Bradley Schmehl. © Somerset
House Publishing. For information on this image call 1-800-444-2540.

American Battlefields
GETTYSBURG
CONTENTS

TWO SOCIETIES: NORTH AND SOUTH

THE BLOODIEST WAR in American history began in April 1861, when southern militia in Charleston, South Carolina, bombarded a U.S. government fort—Fort Sumter— into surrender. The attack came after decades of growing frustration, disagreement, and rage between the northern and southern states.

Through the first half of the 1800s, the northern and southern United States developed into different kinds of societies. The North grew rapidly, fueled by westward expansion, industrialization, and millions of immigrants who crowded into northeastern cities such as Boston. White settlers moved west, clearing the forests to plant crops. Workers found jobs in factories that produced tons of goods, especially cloth. Railroads were laid out to knit the new markets together.

In contrast, southern society was based on agriculture. Southern farmers planted crops, such as cotton, and sold them to northern and European factories. Large farms, known as plantations, dominated southern agriculture. African slaves worked the fields and performed the many chores needed to keep the plantations running. In 1808, Congress, the nation's highest lawmaking body, had made it illegal to import slaves into the United States. Slaves were still openly traded

An 1861 lithograph depicts the bombardment of Fort Sumter in Charleston Harbor.

and sold within the "slave states"—states that allowed slavery—however. Most of the South's political leaders owned slaves.

As the United States expanded westward, politicians worked carefully to preserve the balance of power in Congress—to maintain an equal number of slave states and "free states," where slavery was illegal. In 1820 Congress made a plan whereby Missouri was admitted into the Union (the United States) as a slave state, and Maine as a free state. Called the Missouri Compromise, the plan also prohibited slavery in the northern half of unsettled territories farther west.

The question of slavery, however, could not be settled by compromises in Congress. A growing number of critics, called abolitionists, protested that slavery was cruel and inhuman. Abolitionists were a small but loud group. Although the abolitionist movement was based in the North, most northern whites did not openly worry about the plight of slaves. Southerners, however, reacted to the criticism with anger.

Even more aggravating to southern slave owners, abolitionists and their supporters ran an "underground railroad." The "railroad" was a network of people and safe places used to smuggle escaped slaves to freedom in the North. In 1850 Congress passed a fugitive (runaway) slave law that required police officers, and even private citizens, to help return runaway slaves to their owners. The law disgusted many northerners and strengthened the antislavery attitude.

"The abolitionism which I advocate is as absolute as the law of God, and as unyielding as his throne. It admits of no compromise. Every slave is a stolen man; every slaveholder is a man stealer. While a slave remains in his fetters, the land must have no rest."[1]
—Abolitionist William Lloyd Garrison, 1854

NAT TURNER'S REBELLION

In 1831 a slave named Nat Turner led seventy-five other slaves in a short but bloody rebellion in Virginia. The slaves killed about sixty whites. White southerners, who had argued that slaves were happy with their condition, were shocked. Many southerners blamed the rebellion on abolitionists.

Black slaves working a cotton plantation on the Mississippi River.

DRIFTING INTO WAR

As the abolitionists grew louder, southerners and northerners continued to argue about the status of slavery in unsettled territories in the West. In 1854 Congress passed an act that gave settlers in the new territories the right to decide whether or not slavery should be allowed there. Called the Kansas-Nebraska Act, this law repealed the 1820 Missouri Compromise, which had prohibited slavery in much of the new territories.

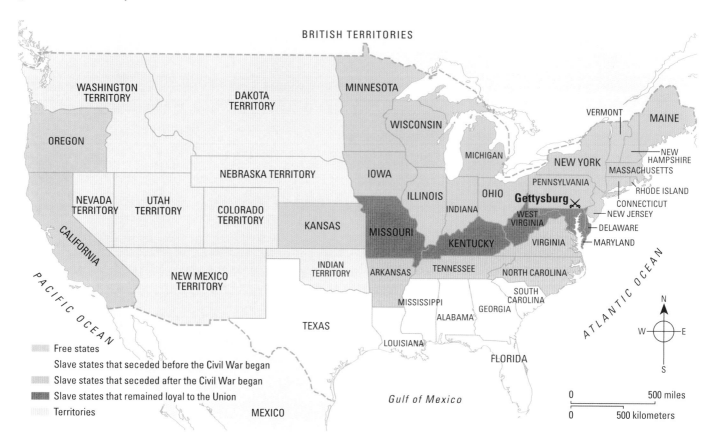

BRITISH TERRITORIES

WASHINGTON TERRITORY

DAKOTA TERRITORY

MINNESOTA

WISCONSIN

VERMONT

MAINE

OREGON

MICHIGAN

NEW YORK

NEW HAMPSHIRE

MASSACHUSETTS

NEBRASKA TERRITORY

IOWA

PENNSYLVANIA

RHODE ISLAND

NEVADA TERRITORY

UTAH TERRITORY

COLORADO TERRITORY

KANSAS

ILLINOIS

INDIANA

OHIO

Gettysburg

CONNECTICUT

NEW JERSEY

CALIFORNIA

MISSOURI

KENTUCKY

WEST VIRGINIA

VIRGINIA

DELAWARE

MARYLAND

NEW MEXICO TERRITORY

INDIAN TERRITORY

ARKANSAS

TENNESSEE

NORTH CAROLINA

ATLANTIC OCEAN

PACIFIC OCEAN

TEXAS

MISSISSIPPI

ALABAMA

GEORGIA

SOUTH CAROLINA

N

W E

LOUISIANA

FLORIDA

S

Free states

Slave states that seceded before the Civil War began

Slave states that seceded after the Civil War began

Slave states that remained loyal to the Union

Territories

MEXICO

Gulf of Mexico

0   500 miles

0   500 kilometers

The law caused an uproar in the North, where white farmers wanted unsettled western lands reserved for them, not for slave owners. In July 1854, antislavery northerners founded a new political group, the Republican Party.

The ugly mood between North and South even led to violence in Congress. On May 22, 1856, a southern congressman, angered by a northern senator's antislavery speech that had named the congressman's relative, used a cane to beat the senator unconscious on the Senate floor.

During the Civil War, eleven slave states left the Union to form the Confederacy. But four slave states remained loyal and fought with the Union, joined only a few weeks before Gettysburg by pro-Union West Virginia, carved out of rebellious Virginia.

Two more events further poisoned relations between North and South. In 1857, in the Dred Scott decision, the Supreme Court ruled that Congress could not prohibit slavery in the territories. The court ruled that slavery was supported by the Constitution. Republicans were horrified by this decision. Then, in 1859, a white northerner named John Brown led an attack on a government arsenal at Harpers Ferry, Virginia. Brown and his small group of followers hoped to incite a slave rebellion that would sweep through the South. The revolt was quickly crushed, and Brown was hanged. But the failed rebellion, and northern sympathy for Brown, terrified and angered southerners.

In 1860 Republican candidate Abraham Lincoln was elected president of the United States. Lincoln, a lawyer from Illinois, said he would prohibit slavery in the western territories. To many southerners, Lincoln's election was too much. Eleven southern states decided to secede, or withdraw, from the Union, banding together as the Confederate States of America. When the Confederates attacked Fort Sumter in South Carolina on April 12, 1861, President Lincoln called for volunteer soldiers to put down the southern rebellion. Thousands eagerly answered his call. The Civil War had begun.

Appealing to a sense of patriotism, recruiting posters encouraged men to volunteer for the Union army.

"If I could save the Union without freeing any slave, I would do it; and if I could save it by freeing all the slaves, I would do it; and if I could save it by freeing some and leaving others alone, I would also do that. What I do about slavery and the colored race I do because I believe it helps to save this Union; and what I forbear, I forbear because I do not believe it would help to save the Union…. I have here stated my purpose according to my view of official duty, and I intend no modification of my oft-expressed personal wish that all men, everywhere could be free."[2]
—Abraham Lincoln to Horace Greeley, editor of the *New York Tribune*, August 1862

Abraham Lincoln in 1860. Lincoln would lead the nation through its bloodiest war.

LEE MARCHES NORTH

Neither side expected the war to last very long. After nearly two years, however, thousands of men had been killed and wounded in terrible battles, and neither side was prepared to give in. In June 1863, Confederate general Robert E. Lee, commander of the Army of Northern Virginia, devised a plan to win the war. He ordered an invasion of the North. A few weeks earlier, Lee had defeated the Union Army of the Potomac in northern Virginia at the Battle of Chancellorsville. His men were confident after their spectacular victory. Lee also hoped to win open European support if he defeated the Union army in Maryland or Pennsylvania. Both France and Great Britain were suffering because the northern navy had cut off most trade between the South and Europe. If France or Great Britain were to enter the war on the side of the South, then Confederate success was assured.

A Union infantryman.

Dead Confederate infantry after bitter fighting at the Battle of Chancellorsville.

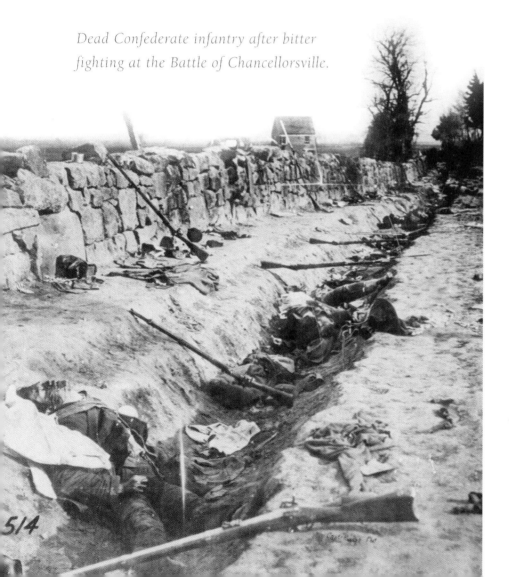

"There's hardly any sickness or straggling in the army.... We have a large army now in Pennsylvania and it is good and in fine spirits. We intend to let the Yankey Nation [Union] feel the sting of the War as our borders [have] ever since the war began."[3]

—Eli Landers, a private in the Sixteenth Georgia Infantry

In mid-June, Confederate infantry crossed the Potomac River, which separated Virginia from Maryland. Lee's 70,000 men marched behind a line of mountains that stretched from Virginia to Pennsylvania. Using the mountains as a screen, Lee planned to keep his movements hidden from Union forces. Lee hoped to be well into Pennsylvania before Union generals realized what was happening.

Union commander Joseph Hooker, however, heard reports of the Confederate movement. He ordered the Army of the Potomac, which consisted of 93,000 men, to pursue. Long columns of Union soldiers and supply wagons packed the roads leading north. Hooker, however, fundamentally disagreed with his commanders in Washington, D.C., the nation's capital, so on June 27, he asked to be removed from command. President Lincoln agreed and appointed George G. Meade to head the Army of the Potomac. When Union soldiers heard of the change, they mostly shrugged. Meade was just one of several new commanders in the past two years.

By then, Confederate soldiers had occupied the town of Chambersburg, Pennsylvania, and threatened the state capital in Harrisburg. On June 27, Lee learned that the Union army had already left Virginia and was advancing north. Surprised by the news, Lee ordered his scattered army to come back together.

"Such a hard looking set I never saw. Thousands are passing—such a rough dirty ragged rowdyish set one does not often see. A body would think the whole south had broke loose & are coming into [Pennsylvania]. It makes me feel too badly to see so many men & cannon going through knowing that they have come to kill our men."4
—Rachel Cormany, a resident of Chambersburg, Pennsylvania, about twenty-five miles west of Gettysburg

WHERE WAS STUART?

In mid-June, Lee's cavalry, commanded by the dashing J. E. B. Stuart, had swung around the Union army and out of contact with the Confederate army. Lee, who relied on his cavalry to determine the size and location of the Union army, was left confused and unsure about enemy forces. Stuart caught up to Lee on July 2, after the Battle of Gettysburg had already started.

The Duplin Grays, a Confederate unit raised from Duplin County, North Carolina, parade in camp in May 1861.

THE GENERALS

ROBERT E. LEE, a Virginia plantation owner, was among the nation's most respected officers when the Civil War began. President Lincoln offered him command of the Union army. But Lee turned Lincoln down because he would not fight against his home state of Virginia. Bold and often ruthless in the attack, Lee had an uncanny ability to read his opponent's mind. Under his leadership, the Confederate army won remarkable victories in Virginia. It drove off Union armies outside Richmond in 1862, smashed a Union army at Bull Run, and repulsed attacks outside Fredericksburg. At Chancellorsville, Lee outmaneuvered and outfought a Union army twice the size of his own.

Lee's army was organized into three groups, called corps, of about 20,000 men each. The First Corps was led by James Longstreet, a North Carolinian and Lee's most experienced and dependable officer. Lee promoted two other men,

Lee put great trust in James Longstreet, who led the First Corps.

FRIENDS AT WAR

Almost all high-ranking Civil War generals, both Union and Confederate, were trained at the U.S. Military Academy at West Point, New York. Many of them were good friends. Lewis A. Armistead and Winfield Hancock had been inseparable at West Point. The two would fight opposite each other at Gettysburg.

General Robert E. Lee was among the most respected commanders in the United States. He turned down command of the Union army to serve the Confederacy.

Richard S. Ewell and A. P. Hill, to take command of the Second and Third Corps. Both men had already proven themselves in battle, but neither had directed a unit as large as a corps before.

George G. Meade was given the task four other Union generals had failed to fulfill—defeat Robert E. Lee. Meade was a capable officer but not considered brilliant. He had a quick temper and was nicknamed "the snapping turtle." The Army of the Potomac was divided into seven corps that ranged in size from 9,000 to 13,000 men each. Several were well led. John Reynolds, among the best fighters in the Union army, commanded the First Corps. Winfield Hancock, nicknamed "the magnificent," directed the Second Corps, a proud unit. Daniel Sickles, commander of the Third Corps, was more reckless. His actions at Gettysburg would bring the Union army to the brink of disaster.

Tough, competent, but irritable, Major-General George Meade (above) was given command of the Union army just days before battle broke out at Gettysburg. Confederate general Lee was respectful when he heard of Meade's appointment, remarking that Meade would commit no blunders in battle.

"Stonewall" Jackson, who died shortly after the Battle of Chancellorsville, had been one of the South's most acclaimed officers.

THE MISSING GENERAL

Through more than a year of battles, Robert E. Lee had relied upon his lieutenant, Thomas "Stonewall" Jackson, to win victories. Jackson, however, was wounded at the Battle of Chancellorsville, shot by his own men who mistook him for the enemy in the darkness. Eight days later, on May 10, 1863, Jackson died. He was deeply mourned in the South.

SOLDIERS' EQUIPMENT

By 1863, both armies were made up largely of veterans who had already experienced combat. During a campaign, a soldier carried only what was necessary. Over his left shoulder, he slung a leather cartridge box that held up to sixty rounds of ammunition. Over his right shoulder, he often carried a pouch to hold food and a canteen of water or coffee. Extra clothing and personal items, such as playing cards or a Bible, were stored in a knapsack or rolled in a blanket. The soldier rested his gun, called a musket, on his shoulder as he marched. He sometimes used his blanket to pad his shoulder.

Most Union soldiers wore uniforms made from wool. The shirt was dark blue and was closed with four brass buttons. The pants were sky blue and were held up by suspenders. Leather shoes, called brogans, laced up over the ankle.

The Confederate soldiers were not as well equipped. Unlike the North, the South didn't have many factories to make shoes, uniforms, and guns. Many Confederate soldiers carried captured Union equipment. Officers and some soldiers wore gray uniforms, but the majority of units were clad in mixed shades of brown, khaki, and butternut.

Soldiers trained to act as a unit. They spent large amounts of time practicing on parade fields packed solid by thousands of marching feet. The men learned to advance in a wide straight line, to retreat, and to pivot left or right. They practiced firing their guns together, in a round of simultaneous shots called a volley.

Because the North had more industry than the South, the typical Union soldier (above) had better clothing and equipment than the typical Confederate (left).

Most Civil War infantrymen carried guns called muzzle loaders—they were loaded from the end of the barrel. To load the gun, the soldier opened his cartridge box and pulled out a paper cartridge, which contained a small amount of gunpowder and a bullet. He bit off the top of the cartridge, poured the gunpowder down the barrel, then pushed the bullet down the barrel with a ramrod. The soldier next placed a small explosive cap on the rifle near the trigger and pulled back the hammer. When the soldier pulled the trigger, the hammer slammed down on the cap, creating a spark that ignited the gunpowder. The gunpowder exploded and sent the bullet spinning down the gun barrel. A well-trained soldier could fire about three rounds a minute.

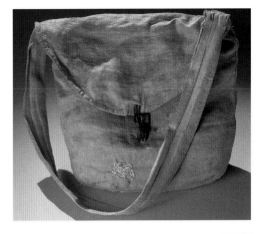

BIG GUNS

Artillery pieces—large firearms such as cannons (below)—were deadly against infantry troops. Artillery could shoot large shells over long distances. At close range, artillery fired shells that exploded into hundreds of deadly pieces. These shells, called canister, devastated masses of enemy soldiers packed together in formation.

An artillery battery consisted of six guns. Each gun was pulled by a team of four horses and was typically manned by a crew of six.

Top: A soldier's haversack, or carrying case. Bottom: A soldier's shaving kit.

THE BATTLEFIELD

THE CONFEDERATE ARMY advanced into the lush farmland of south-central Pennsylvania. It was a welcome change from northern Virginia, where two years of war had left the countryside ravaged and bare. The Confederate soldiers seized animals from the rich Pennsylvania farms and helped themselves to goods stocked in town stores with delight. They often paid, but with worthless Confederate money. The townspeople mostly waited in nervous quiet behind locked doors or peeked through shade-drawn windows. Local militias, made up mostly of untrained boys or older men, organized to resist the Rebels. They usually scattered before the advance of Lee's infantry.

As the Confederate forces marched into Pennsylvania, the Army of the Potomac approached from the south, keeping themselves between the Confederates and Washington, D.C. The town of Gettysburg, with ten roads running through it, occupied a central location between the two armies.

Most Pennsylvania store owners were dismayed when Confederate soldiers paid for goods with Confederate money. This Confederate $500 note carried a picture of General Stonewall Jackson.

The town of Gettysburg, July 1863.

On June 30, a Confederate force commanded by J. Johnston Pettigrew approached Gettysburg from the west. The Confederates spotted horsemen, and Pettigrew, who was under strict orders not to begin a battle, withdrew. That evening Pettigrew reported that Union cavalrymen were in Gettysburg and that strong Union infantry could be close by. Confederate officers Henry Heth and A. P. Hill didn't believe the report. When Heth asked if he could send his infantry into Gettysburg the next morning, Hill agreed.

Unknown to Heth, the horsemen were Union cavalry, commanded by John Buford, and Union infantry troops were in fact just a few hours away. Buford knew the Confederates would return on July 1. He was determined to keep them from occupying Gettysburg. He posted his 2,750 soldiers on the roads west and north of the town. He gave his men a warning. "You will have to fight like the devil to hold your own until [infantry] supports arrive."[5]

"The enemy are on our soil; the whole country now looks anxiously to this army to deliver it from the presence of the foe; our failure to do so will leave us no such welcome as the swelling of millions of hearts with pride and joy at our success would give to every soldier of this army. Homes, firesides, and domestic altars are involved. The enemy has fought well heretofore; it is believed that it will fight more desperately and bravely than ever."[6]

—General George G. Meade,
June 30, 1863

A company of Union infantry, in full uniform and with bayonets fixed, stands in two ranks. This regiment is part of the Third Corps, identified by a diamond patch stitched onto the soldiers' hats. The patch is clearly visible on the hat worn by the soldier standing at the left end of the rear rank (behind the drummer).

THE FIRST DAY

Just after dawn on July 1, 1863, John Buford's dismounted cavalry northwest of Gettysburg spotted shadowy figures approaching. The men took aim and fired. Gunshots broke the morning stillness as Buford's men fought stubbornly against Henry Heth's soldiers. Several miles to the south, Union general John Reynolds led his First Corps toward the sounds of battle.

Marching at double quick, his panting men reached McPherson Ridge, a low ridge west of Gettysburg. They arrived just as the Union cavalrymen were about to be overwhelmed by Confederate infantry. The Union "Iron Brigade," a famed unit of tough soldiers from the Midwest, approached a line of trees. "Forward men, forward, for God's sake, and drive those fellows out of the woods!" cried Reynolds.[7] The Iron Brigade fired into the surprised Confederates, then hurried to take hundreds of prisoners, including brigade commander James J. Archer. All along McPherson Ridge, the Confederate attack stalled.

"Why we failed to push on and occupy the heights around and beyond Gettysburg is one of the unsettled questions. Our army expected to do so and were disappointed when we did not."[8]
—William Fulton, a private in James J. Archer's brigade

Union forces stood north of Gettysburg in the afternoon, just before advancing Confederates drove them in disorder back through town.

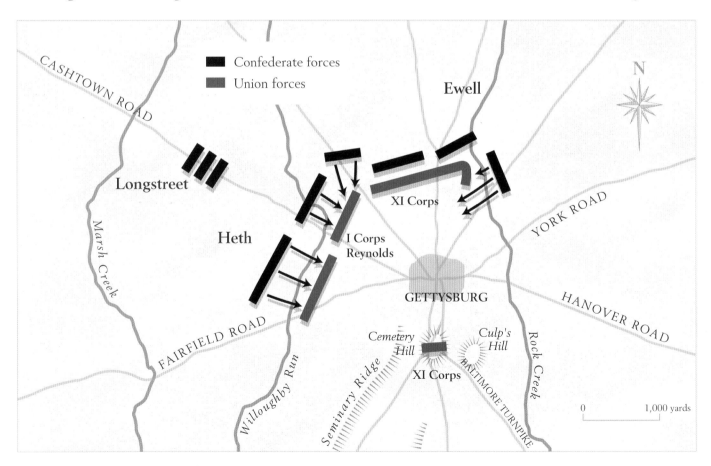

Confederate forces
Union forces

CASHTOWN ROAD

Ewell

N

Longstreet

Marsh Creek

Heth

XI Corps

I Corps Reynolds

YORK ROAD

GETTYSBURG

HANOVER ROAD

FAIRFIELD ROAD

Willoughby Run

Seminary Ridge

Cemetery Hill

Culp's Hill

XI Corps

Rock Creek

BALTIMORE TURNPIKE

0   1,000 yards

Both armies rushed reinforcements to Gettysburg. The Union Eleventh Corps took positions on the right of the First Corps and faced north. About 3:00 p.m. Richard Ewell's forces attacked them. A brigade of a thousand Georgians, hollering and yipping the "Rebel yell," crashed into the right end of the Union line. Hit on two sides, the Union soldiers retreated in confusion.

At the same moment, a fresh brigade of North Carolina men advanced into McPherson Woods. The Confederate troops and the Iron Brigade pounded each other with volleys. The Union position, manned by exhausted soldiers who had fought since morning, crumbled. Union soldiers streamed back through Gettysburg, jamming the streets as cannon shells exploded overhead.

The survivors gathered on a rise called Cemetery Hill, just south of Gettysburg. Lee carefully scanned this new position through his binoculars. He sent a note to Ewell, directing him to attack if he felt his troops could succeed. Ewell was confused by the order. Believing his troops were exhausted, he delayed and then decided against the attack. Lee felt that a second day of battle was needed. "If the enemy is there tomorrow, we must attack him," he said.[9]

Union artillery is rushed into battle.

Confederate soldiers unhinged the Union line north of Gettysburg. This painting depicts desperate Union regiments of the Eleventh Corps retreating to the outskirts of the town as the Confederate attack rolls over them.

THE SECOND DAY

On July 2, General Meade discovered that the countryside outside Gettysburg offered a strong defensive position. The Union line was shaped like a fishhook. Starting on the wooded Culp's Hill, it curled around Cemetery Hill and down Cemetery Ridge before ending on a rocky, cleared hill called Little Round Top.

General Lee, determined to crush the Union army, ordered James Longstreet to strike the left Union flank (left side of the line). Longstreet struggled to get his troops into position, however. In the meantime, the left end of the Union line shifted. Union general Dan Sickles moved his Third Corps out from Cemetery Ridge, a position he thought was weak, to higher ground near a peach orchard. But the move left Sickles's men stretched thin. Little Round Top was now unoccupied. If the Confederates could capture Little Round Top, they could bombard the Union line with cannon fire.

At 3:40 p.m., Longstreet's men finally attacked. The cheering Confederates dislodged Union troops from a rocky rise called

A RELUCTANT GENERAL?

At Gettysburg, James Longstreet argued that Lee should not send Confederate soldiers into bloody attacks against dug-in Union positions. "[The enemy] is anxious we attack him," Longstreet told Lee.[10] Longstreet urged Lee to withdraw instead, and force the Union army to attack the Confederates. After the battle, Longstreet was accused of not obeying Lee's July 2 orders properly.

Longstreet hit the exposed Union Third Corps in the south. Late in the day, Confederates struck the right side of the Union line farther north.

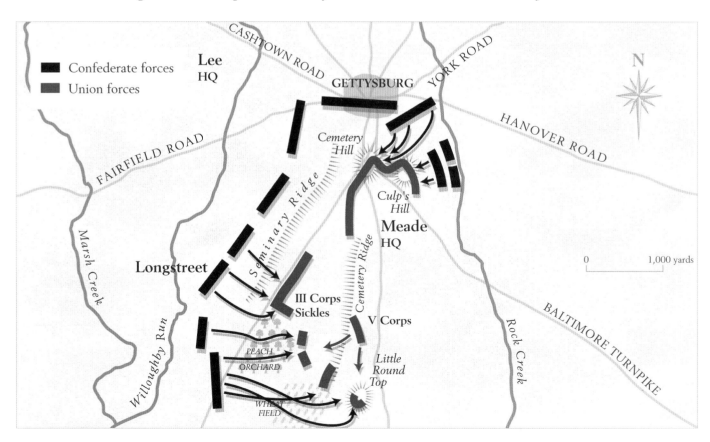

Devil's Den, captured three cannons, and swarmed into the valley beneath Little Round Top. Moments before, Union officer Gouverneur Warren had noticed that Little Round Top was unoccupied. He frantically ordered nearby units to the top. Soon after the Union soldiers filed into position, red Confederate battle flags appeared on the crest.

In desperation, the Union and Confederate soldiers fired at each other. On the left side, the Twentieth Maine stood among trees and boulders to fight off repeated Confederate charges. "The fire was so destructive that my line wavered like a man trying to walk against a strong wind,"[11] recalled a Confederate colonel.

At the peach orchard, a unit of Mississippi soldiers smashed the Union line, sending crowds of men and horse-drawn cannons hurrying to the rear. Meade rushed in reinforcements. An area known as the Wheat Field became an inferno of musket fire. It was captured and lost six times. The Confederate advance crested on Cemetery Ridge and fell back, exhausted. The Confederates then attacked Culp's Hill and Cemetery Hill, mostly failing against the dug-in Union defenders.

It had been some of the most savage fighting of the war. In six hours, almost 17,000 men on both sides had been killed or wounded. The Union army, however, still held most of its positions. Lee planned for a third day of fighting.

These Confederate soldiers were killed while attacking across the rocky landscape of Devil's Den.

Artist Alfred Waud sketched combat from a close-up battlefield location. The print on the bottom left, based on a Waud sketch, shows Confederate soldiers driving Union troops from Devil's Den.

PICKETT'S CHARGE

On the morning of July 3, General Lee ordered a grand assault upon the center of the Union line on Cemetery Ridge. He believed the attack would smash the Union army and end the war. At about noon, more than 140 Confederate cannons were wheeled into position to blast the Union troops. At 1:00 p.m., they opened fire in thunderous cannonade.

For two hours, the guns pounded the Union lines. The Confederate gunners aimed too high, however, and most of their shells whistled harmlessly overhead. When the cannon fire ended, General George E. Pickett led more than 12,000 Confederate soldiers in thick ranks toward Cemetery Ridge.

The Confederate lines stretched across the open valley floor. To Union artillerymen on the ridge, the enemy infantry offered a perfect target. When the Confederates drew within 100 yards, the Union soldiers rose and fired a shattering volley into the attackers. Two Union regiments swung out around the Confederate force and raked its flanks.

"Even now I can hear them cheering as I gave the order, 'Forward!' I can feel the thrill of their joyous voices as they called out all along the line, 'We'll follow you, Master George. We'll follow you, we'll follow you.' Oh, how faithfully they kept their word, following me on, on to their death, and I, believing in the promised support, led them on, on, on."[12]

—George E. Pickett, in a letter to his fiancée three days after the battle

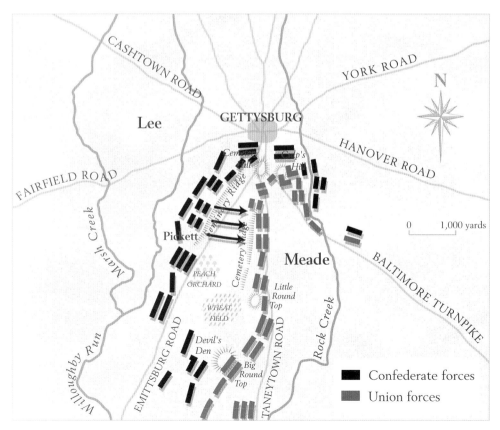

Lee sent his remaining fresh troops against the center of the Union line on Cemetery Ridge.

THE ONLY CIVILIAN DEATH

On the morning of July 3, Jennie Wade was baking bread in a Gettysburg home between the Union and Confederate lines when a stray bullet pierced two doors and struck her. Wade, just twenty years old, was killed instantly. She was the only civilian death in the battle.

Facing devastating musket fire on three sides, Pickett's Charge began to collapse. A small group of Confederates, led by Lewis Armistead, broke into the Union lines. Soldiers swung their rifles like clubs, officers fired their pistols at close range, men grappled desperately in hand-to-hand combat. Fresh Union regiments appeared and fired into the mass. Armistead fell, hit by several bullets. He and most of his men were captured.

The survivors streamed back to the Confederate positions, where General Lee rode out among them. He spotted General Pickett and ordered him to prepare his division for a counterattack. "General Lee," Pickett answered, "I have no division."[13]

"I tell you there is no romance in making one of these charges. I tell you the ardent enthusiasm in many cases ain't there, and instead of burning to avenge the insults of our country, families, and altars and firesides, the thought is most frequently, Oh, if I could just come out of this charge safely how thankful I would be!"[14]

—John Dooley, First Virginia Infantry

A scene from the Gettysburg cyclorama showing savage fighting during Pickett's Charge.

RETREAT AND PURSUIT

George Meade's army was as exhausted in victory as the Confederate force was in defeat. Meade launched no counterattack. That evening, Robert E. Lee ordered his army to retreat. The Battle of Gettysburg was over, and all Lee's hopes for a Confederate victory that summer were dashed.

"It has been a sad, sad day to us," Lee told a cavalry officer that night. "I never saw troops behave more magnificently than Pickett's division of Virginians did today in that grand charge upon the enemy. And if they had been supported, we would have held the position and the day would have been ours. Too bad! Too bad! Oh! Too bad!"[15]

On July 4, Independence Day, a tremendous rainstorm broke, soaking both armies. On July 5, the Confederates slipped out of their positions to begin the long march home to Virginia. The wagon train carrying the thousands of wounded men, who bounced in agony over rutted roads, stretched seventeen miles.

General Meade, who had been commanding the Army of the Potomac for little more than a week, moved slowly after them.

> *"Glorious news! We have won the victory, thank God, and the Rebel Army is fleeing to Virginia. We have thousands of prisoners. This morning our Corps (the 6th) started in pursuit of Lee's Army. We have had rain and the roads are bad, so we move slow. Every house we see is a hospital, and the road is covered with arms and equipment thrown away by the Rebels."[16]*
> —Elisha Hunt Rhodes, Second Rhode Island Infantry, writing in his diary on July 5

Meade's headquarters in the aftermath of the Battle of Gettysburg.

In Washington, D.C., President Lincoln waited impatiently. He had learned of the victory at Gettysburg. Now he hoped to hear that Lee's army had been destroyed. "You have given the enemy a stunning blow at Gettysburg," Lincoln told Meade through his staff. "Follow it up, and give him another before he can reach the Potomac."[17]

Meade, however, only harassed the Confederate columns. Lee's army was left largely alone. By July 14, the last Confederate troops had crossed into the safety of Virginia. The campaign was over.

General Lee took responsibility for the failure to win at Gettysburg. Shortly after the battle, he offered his resignation to Confederate president Jefferson Davis. Davis refused it, however. Lee remained in command of the Army of Northern Virginia.

Meade's army crosses the Potomac River on July 21, in slow pursuit of Lee's army.

A nurse attends to wounded Union soldiers in a hospital in Nashville, Tennessee.

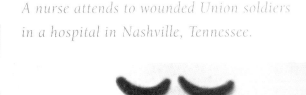

"We know the Rebels are retreating, and that our army has been victorious. I was anxious to help care for the wounded, but the day is ended and all is quiet, and for the first time in a week I shall go to bed, feeling safe."[18]
—Sarah Broadhead, Gettysburg resident, writing in her diary on July 5

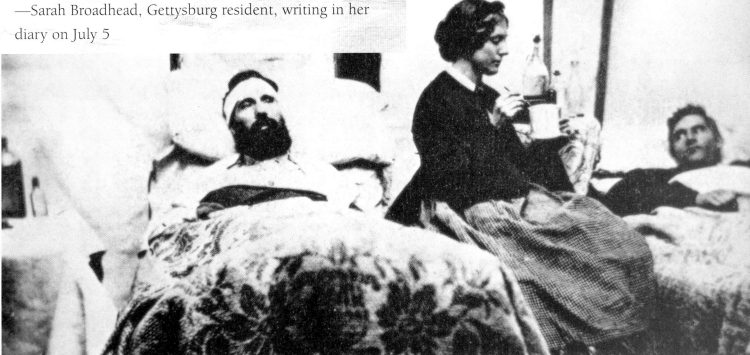

THE COST

In the months after the battle, Gettysburg became a vast military hospital. Churches, barns, and homes were crammed with thousands of wounded and dying men. Work parties carrying shovels and pickaxes buried the thousands of corpses scattered through the woods and fields.

The cost of the battle had been enormous. Of the 75,000 Confederates who had marched north, between 21,000 and 27,000 had become casualties, with an estimated 4,500 killed. Worse, the Confederates lost enormous numbers of officers, and many of their veteran units were effectively destroyed.

The Union also suffered grievously: 23,050 total casualties—3,155 killed, 14,530 wounded, 5,365 missing. The First Corps

"Crossing the battlefield—Cemitary Hill—The Great Wheat Field Farm, Seminary ridge—and other places where dead men, horses, smashed artillery, were strewn in utter confusion, the Blue and the Grey mixed—Their bodies so bloated—distorted—discolored on account of decomposition having set in—that they were utterly unrecognizable, save by clothing, or things in their pockets—The scene simply beggars description."[19]
—Samuel Cormany, Union cavalryman, writing on July 5

These three men were among thousands of Confederates taken prisoner during the Gettysburg campaign. The photograph shows how typical Confederate soldiers dressed. The man in the center is wearing a blanket roll.

and the Third Corps never recovered from the fighting at Gettysburg. Rufus Dawes, who fought with the Iron Brigade, wrote to his sister on July 6: "The experience of the past few days seem more like a horrible dream than the reality. May God save me and my men from any more such trials."[20]

Today, the Battle of Gettysburg is called the high-water mark, or turning point, in the Civil War. When Pickett's men began their attack, the South stood at its greatest strength. Afterward, however, Lee would never again have such a powerful force. "We came here with the best army the Confederacy ever carried into the field but thousands of our brave boys are left upon the enemy's soil and in my opinion our Army will never be made up of such material again," wrote a South Carolina soldier.[21]

After the battle, the Confederacy fought on bravely and stubbornly, but with dwindling numbers of men, ammunition, and supplies. On April 9, 1865, General Lee surrendered the Army of Northern Virginia at Appomattox Courthouse, Virginia, effectively ending the Civil War.

This picture of scattered Union dead shows the ferocity of the fighting around Gettysburg.

A painting of Lee's surrender at Appomattox Courthouse.

THE GETTYSBURG ADDRESS

UNION BURIAL parties reached most of the dead within a week after the battle. The graves were mostly dug where the soldiers had fallen, however, and were scattered over the battlefield. Many were shallow and washed open by rains. Some were marked with a simple wooden board, carrying the name, rank, and unit of the buried man. Others had no identification at all.

Many Gettysburg residents, and the governor of Pennsylvania, Andrew Curtin, were distressed by the shallow and poorly tended Union graves. They developed a plan to create a new soldiers' cemetery on Gettysburg's Cemetery Hill, which so many Union soldiers had died defending. Curtin pledged to support the project with Pennsylvania state money. An architect laid out the cemetery, called the Soldiers National Cemetery, arranging the graves according to the soldiers' home states.

Crews bury the dead of both sides who were killed during the battle.

Gettysburg lawyer David Wills invited several officials to speak at the opening of the cemetery. Wills sent a letter to President Lincoln, inviting him to give "a few appropriate remarks."[22] To Wills's surprise, Lincoln agreed to come.

On November 19, 1863, with the scars of the battle still clear in the surrounding landscape, thousands of people gathered at the cemetery. President Lincoln spoke for little more than two minutes. His remarks, called the Gettysburg Address, are remembered as one of his greatest speeches. Lincoln summarized the struggle for which the soldiers had died—that the "government of the people, by the people, for the people, shall not perish from the earth."

Another speaker, Harvard University president Edward Everett, spoke for two hours. He later wrote to President Lincoln: "I should be glad if I could flatter myself that I came as near to the central idea of the occasion in two hours, as you did in two minutes."[23]

This photograph of President Lincoln was taken four days before he delivered the Gettysburg Address.

"*The world will little note, nor long remember what we say here, but it can never forget what they did here. It is for us the living, rather, to be dedicated here to the unfinished work which they who fought here have thus far so nobly advanced. It is rather for us to be here dedicated to the great task remaining before us—that from these honored dead we take increased devotion to that cause for which they gave the last full measure of devotion—that we here highly resolve that these dead shall not have died in vain—that this nation, under God, shall have a new birth of freedom—and that government of the people, by the people, for the people, shall not perish from the earth.*"

—Abraham Lincoln, portion of the Gettysburg Address, November 19, 1863

Lincoln's Gettysburg Address is one of the most admired speeches in modern history. Printers created souvenir copies of the text, such as this elaborate example.

THE MILITARY PARK

The Soldiers National Cemetery was completed in 1872. Twenty-three years later, Congress established the Gettysburg National Military Park at the battlefield. Today, the 6,000-acre park is one of the most visited historic sites in North America, with almost 2 million visitors every year. Over the past two decades, the National Park Service has cleared underbrush and trees in an attempt to restore the landscape to its 1863 appearance.

More than 1,400 stone and bronze memorials dot the park. They line avenues, sit in yards, and stand alone in the woods. They recognize generals, regiments, and even some civilians who played a part in the battle. The first memorial was erected in 1867, when the First Minnesota Infantry placed an urn in the cemetery to honor its fallen comrades. Almost every Union unit that fought at Gettysburg followed suit. As the bitter memories of the war faded, former Confederate states also erected monuments at Gettysburg. Today, the Confederate memorials mostly line Seminary Ridge, where Confederate forces began

"Nearly all of the men had said their good-byes and headed for home. On the station platform a former Union soldier from Oregon and a Louisiana Confederate were taking leave of each other. They shook hands and embraced, but neither seemed able to find the words to express his feelings. Then an idea seemed to strike both men at once. In a simple act, which seemed to say everything they felt the pair took off their uniforms and exchanged them. The Yankee [Union veteran] went home in Rebel gray, the Confederate in Union blue."[24]
—*Eyewitness to the fiftieth anniversary, 1913*

Gettysburg today is crowded with monuments and memorials. This monument, located on Cemetery Ridge, is dedicated to the Pennsylvania soldiers who fought in the Civil War.

REUNION

In 1913 every surviving Civil War soldier was invited to a reunion at Gettysburg to celebrate the fiftieth anniversary of the battle. More than 50,000 veterans attended, staying in a vast camp of canvas tents built for them. Many dressed in their old uniforms and swapped stories with other veterans. On July 3, the Union and Confederate veterans of Pickett's Charge reenacted the assault. This time, as old men, the opponents shook hands over the wall where as young men they had shot and clubbed each other fifty years earlier.

their attacks on July 2 and July 3. A bronze statue of Robert E. Lee, mounted on a horse, stands atop the Virginia monument and gazes toward Cemetery Ridge.

The park also contains one monument not to war and sacrifice but to peace. In 1938, on the seventy-fifth anniversary of the Battle of Gettysburg, President Franklin Delano Roosevelt dedicated the Eternal Light Peace Memorial to everlasting friendship between North and South.

No longer adversaries, a former Union and former Confederate soldier shake hands at a Gettysburg reunion.

A reenactment of the Battle of Gettysburg, held on the 135th anniversary of the battle, drew more than 10,000 reenactors. The scene gives us a colorful glimpse of what a Civil War army looked like. The photograph shows Union soldiers holding firm on Cemetery Ridge after Pickett's Charge.

TIMELINE

1820: Congress passes the Missouri Compromise, which prohibits slavery in most of the western territories.

1830–1860: The northern abolitionist movement grows. The underground railroad helps escaped slaves find safety in northern states and Canada.

1850: Congress passes a fugitive slave law.

1854: Congress passes the Kansas-Nebraska Act, which repeals the Missouri Compromise.

1860: Abraham Lincoln is elected president; South Carolina is the first state to secede from the Union.

1861: South Carolina and several other southern states form the Confederate States of America; Fort Sumter is bombarded; the Civil War begins.

1863: *May 1–3:* General Hooker is defeated by General Lee at the battle of Chancellorsville.
June 3: Under Lee's orders, Confederate infantry begins marching north.
June 15: Confederate infantry crosses over the Potomac River into Maryland.
June 30: John Buford posts his cavalry soldiers north and west of Gettysburg.
July 1: The Union First and Eleventh Corps battle Confederates north and west of Gettysburg. They are driven through the town and establish a new line on Cemetery Hill.
July 2: The Confederate army attacks Union right and left flanks but fails to achieve a decisive breakthrough.
July 3: Lee orders a massive assault on the center of the Union line. The Confederates penetrate the Union positions but fail to hold.
July 5: Lee's army leaves the Gettysburg area. Meade orders a cautious pursuit.
July 13: The last element of Lee's army retires across the Potomac River to the safety of Virginia. The war will go on.
November 19: Abraham Lincoln gives the Gettysburg Address at the opening of the cemetery for Union soldiers killed in the battle.

1865: Lee surrenders his army at Appomattox Courthouse, Virginia; President Lincoln is assassinated at Ford's Theatre in Washington, D.C.

1872: The Soldiers' National Cemetery is completed.

1895: Congress establishes the Gettysburg National Military Park.

GLOSSARY

abolitionist—a person who opposes slavery and argues for its destruction

artillery—large, heavy guns mounted on wheels that are used to fire large shells at enemy soldiers, artillery, or fortifications

casualty—a soldier who is killed, wounded, or missing after combat

cavalry—army units that are mounted on horses

flank—the right or left side of an army's position

infantry—soldiers who are armed and equipped to fight on foot

militia—a group of citizens organized for military service

reinforcements—fresh units sent in to strengthen troops in battle

secede—to withdraw from, or officially leave, an organization

veteran—a soldier with previous military experience, especially combat experience

volley—a group of shots fired by soldiers all at the same time

FURTHER INFORMATION

BOOKS TO READ

Catton, Bruce. *Gettysburg: The Final Fury.* New York: Doubleday, 1974.

Foote, Shelby. *Stars in Their Courses: The Gettysburg Campaign.* New York: Modern Library, 1994.

Freedman, Russell. *Lincoln: A Photobiography.* New York: Clarion Books, 1988.

Kantor, MacKinlay. *Gettysburg.* New York: Random House Children's Books, 1987.

Murphy, Jim. *The Long Road to Gettysburg.* New York: Clarion Books, 2000.

Trudeau, Noah Andre. *Gettysburg: A Testing of Courage.* New York: HarperCollins, 2002.

PLACES TO VISIT

Ford's Theatre National Historic Site, Washington, D.C. *http://www.nps.gov/foth/index2.htm*

Fredericksburg and Spotsylvania National Military Park, Virginia *http://www.nps.gov/frsp/vc.htm*

Gettysburg National Military Park, Gettysburg, Pennsylvania *http://www.nps.gov/gett/index.htm*

WEBSITES

To view more of Bradley Schmehl's historical artwork (see page 17) go to *http://www.bradleyschmehl.biz*

Symbols of Honor: Civil War Flags in National Park Service Collections *http://www.cr.nps.gov/museum/exhibits/flags/*

Camp Life: Civil War Collections from Gettysburg National Military Park *http://www.cr.nps.gov/museum/exhibits/gettex/*

Civil War: Soldiers and Sailors System *http://www.itd.nps.gov/cwss/index.html*

Civil War-Related Sites in the National Park System *http://www.itd.nps.gov/cwss/parks.htm*

NOTES

1. William Safire, ed., *Lend Me Your Ears, Great Speeches in History* (New York: W. W. Norton and Company, 1997).

2. James W. Loewen, *Lies My Teacher Told Me: Everything Your American History Textbook Got Wrong* (New York: Simon and Schuster, 1996).

3. Gettysburg National Military Park Virtual Tour. September 1998. www.nps.gov/gett/getttour/main-ms.htm.

4. James C. Mohr, ed., *The Cormany Diaries: A Northern Family in the Civil War* (Pittsburgh, University of Pittsburgh Press, 1982).

5. Noah Andre Trudeau, *Gettysburg: A Testing of Courage* (New York: HarperCollins Publishers, Inc., 2002), p. 148.

6. The Meade Archive. January 2000. http://adams.patriot.net/~jcampi/meadetest.htm.

7. Trudeau, *Gettysburg*, p. 184.

8. Trudeau, *Gettysburg*, p. 257.

9. Trudeau, *Gettysburg*, p. 252.

10. Ibid.

11. Gettysburg National Military Park Virtual Tour. September 1998. www.nps.gov/gett/getttour/tstops/tstd2-10.htm.

12. The Battle of Gettysburg: The Bloodiest Battle in the Civil War. March 2000. www.thinkspot.net/Gettysburg/LeadersinCon.html.

13. Gettysburg National Military Park Virtual Tour. September 1998. www.nps.gov/gett/getttour/sidebar/pickett.htm.

14. Trudeau, *Gettysburg*, p. 476.

15. Eye Witness—History through the Eyes of Those Who Lived It. June 2003. www.ibiscom.com/gtburg2.htm.

16. Teaching with Historic Places. October 2002. www.cr.nps.gov/nr/twhp/wwwlps/lessons/44gettys/44facts2.htm.

17. Essays and Articles Written by Members of Antietam or History Discussion Group and Friends. n.d. www.bytenet.net/history/2antieta.html.

18. Trudeau, *Gettysburg*, p. 540.

19. Mohr, *The Cormany Diaries*.

20. Gettysburg National Military Park Virtual Tour. September 1998. www.nps.gov/gett/getttour/sidebar/dawes.htm.

21. Trudeau, *Gettysburg*, p. 550.

22. Gettysburg Address. May 2003. www.loc.gov/exhibits/gadd/gainv1.html.

23. Gettysburg National Military Park Virtual Tour. September 1998. www.nps.gov/gett/getttour/tstops/tstd4-23dd.htm.

24. Abbott M. Gibney, "Gettysburg: The 50th Anniversary Encampment," *Civil War Times Illustrated*, October 1970.

INDEX